JEANETTE WINTER

MAMA: A TRUE STORY
in which a BABY HIPPO loses his MAMA
during a TSUNAMI, but finds a new home,
and a new MAMA

HARCOURT, INC.
Orlando   Austin   New York   San Diego   Toronto   London

www.HarcourtBooks.com

Library of Congress Cataloging-in-Publication Data
Winter, Jeanette.
Mama: a true story in which a baby hippo loses his mama during a tsunami
but finds a new home and a new mama/Jeanette Winter.
p. cm.
1. Hippopotamus—Infancy—Juvenile literature.   2. Parental behavior in animals—Juvenile literature.
3. Tsunamis—Environmental aspects—Juvenile literature.   I. Title.
QL737.U57W57 2006
599.63'5139—dc22   2005020905
ISBN-13: 978-0152-05495-3 ISBN-10: 0-15-205495-2

C E G H F D B

Manufactured in China

The illustrations in this book were done in acrylic on Arches watercolor paper.
The display type was set in Oz Poster.
The text lettering was created by Judythe Sieck.
Color separations by Bright Arts Ltd., Hong Kong
Manufactured by South China Printing Company, Ltd., China
This book was printed on totally chlorine-free Stora Enso Matte paper.
Production supervision by Ginger Boyer
Designed by Judythe Sieck

To Ann Cameron

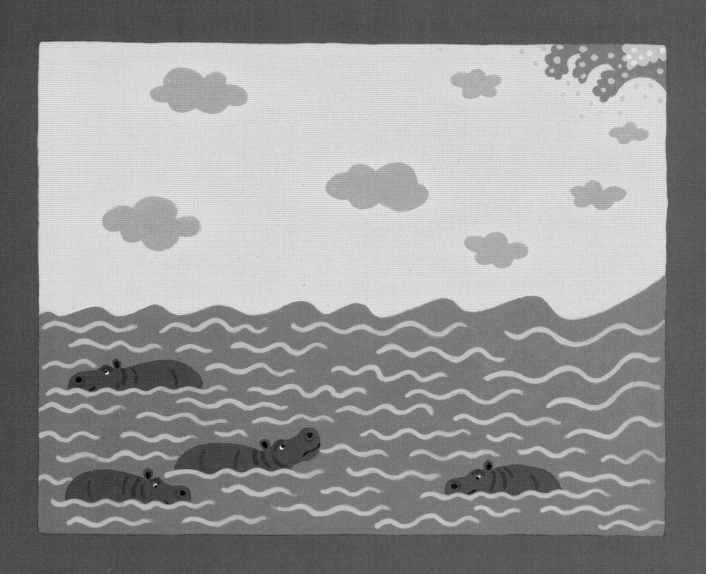

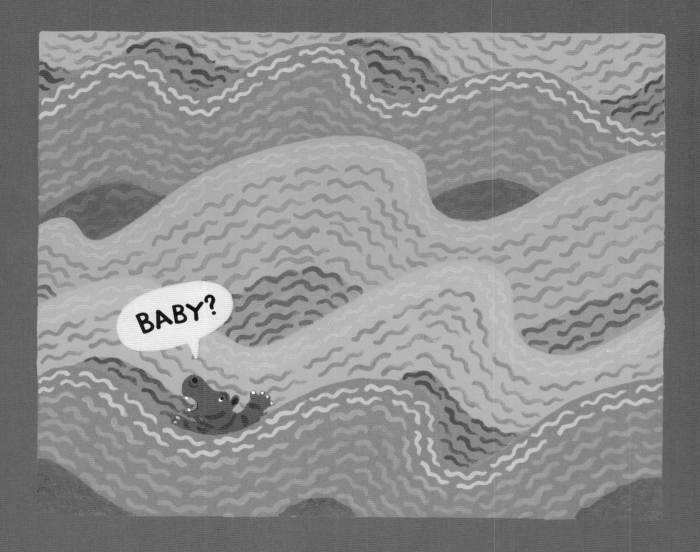

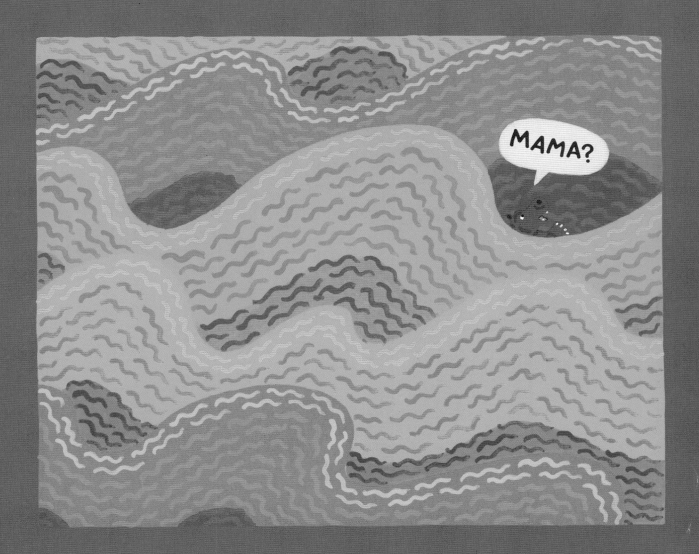

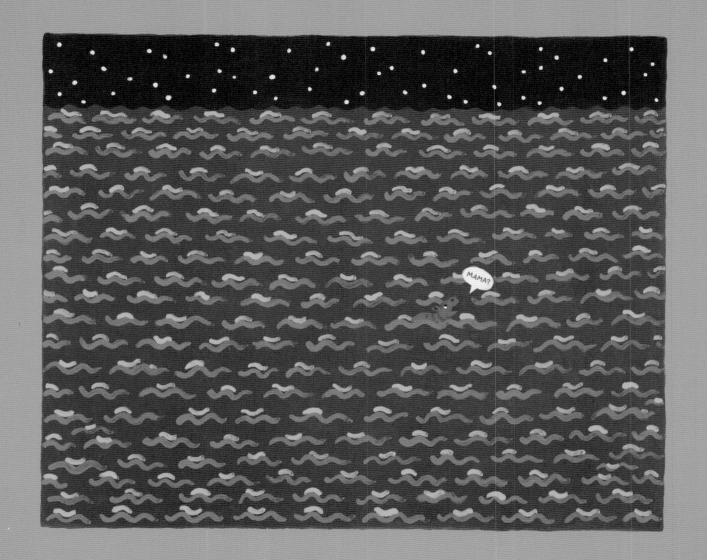

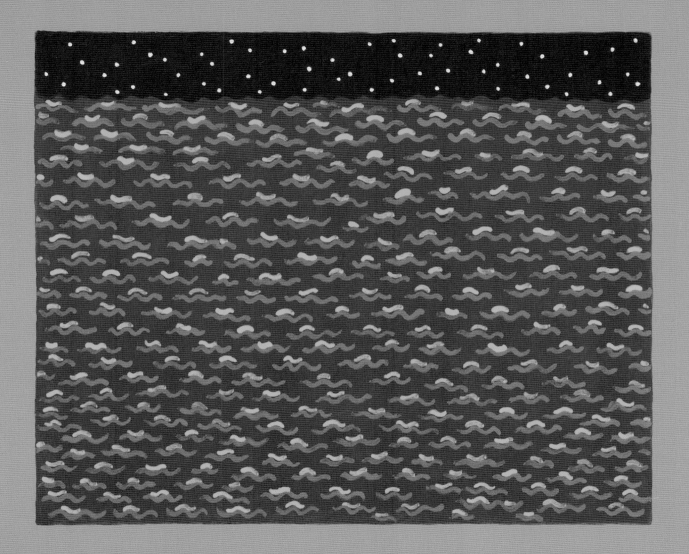

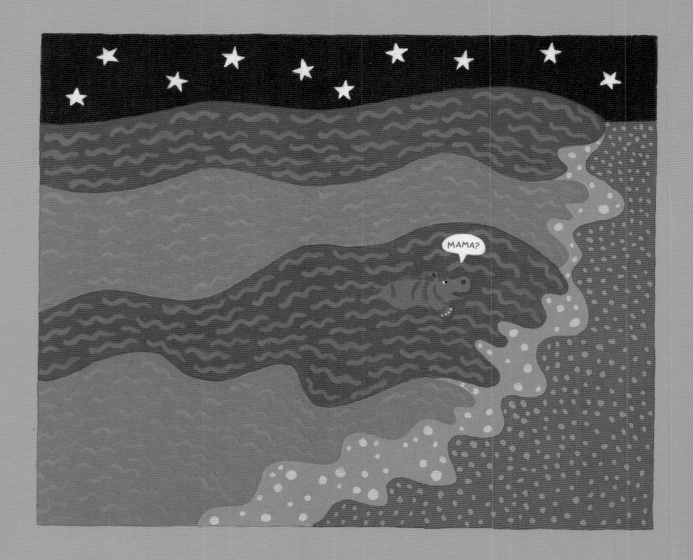

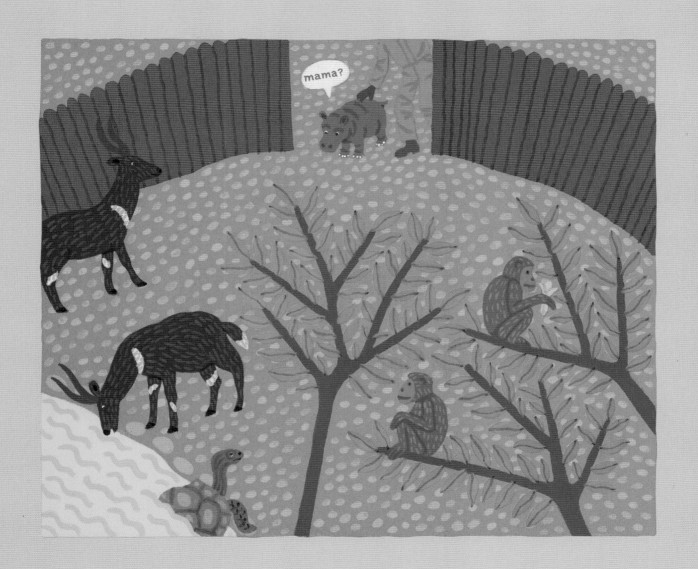

A NOTE FROM THE AUTHOR

On December 26, 2004, a tsunami struck in the Indian Ocean near Indonesia. The resulting high seas caused a group of hippos that were swimming in Kenya's Sabaki River to be swept out to sea.

Most of the hippos made it back to the river safely, but a baby hippo was separated from his mother and the group. After a lonely night in the ocean, the hippo washed up near Malindi.

Kenyan wildlife officials and local fishermen discovered the lost hippo, less than a year old and weighing more than 650 pounds. They named him Owen and brought him to Haller Park in Mombasa, about fifty miles away. Owen was released into an enclosure with several other animals. Almost immediately, he headed for Mzee, a 130-year-old male giant tortoise. (*Mzee* means "old man" in Swahili.)

Soon the two were inseparable. Mzee took on the role of "mama," and despite his harrowing experience, Owen seems quite content.

The park staff hopes that when Owen is older, Cleo, a lonesome twelve-year-old hippo living there, will catch his eye.